3/96

Mountains

Charles Rotter

Creative Education

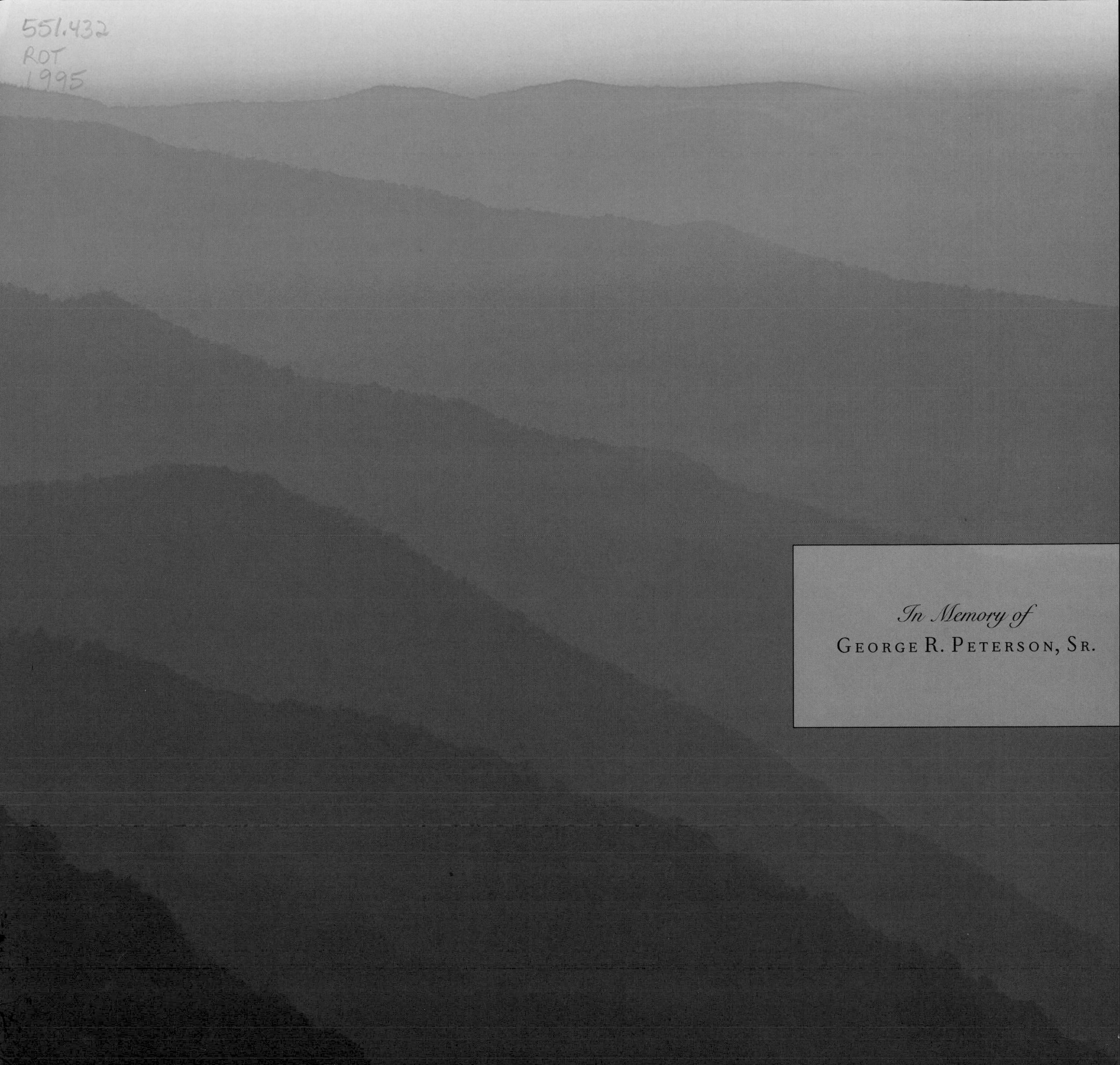

In Memory of
GEORGE R. PETERSON, SR.

7

Mountains are among the most striking landforms on earth. Found on every continent, mountains may stand alone, or as a group they may stretch for thousands of miles. They have influenced the course of history, determining settlement patterns of the world's civilizations and causing wars to be won or lost. In ancient times, mountains were thought to be the homes of gods, and even today mountain climbers defy death to scale the lofty peaks. Indeed, as we approach the twenty-first century, mountains continue to be a compelling symbol of nature's majesty and human aspiration.

Palisade Crest, Kings Canyon National Park, California.

9

What is a mountain? A common definition is any physical feature on the face of the earth that rises more than 1,000 feet (305 m) above the surrounding landscape. But a definition for mountains may take other factors into account as well. A landform's steepness, or *Relief,* is a significant factor, as the steeper a landform's slope, the more likely it will be considered a mountain. Perhaps the most important way to define a mountain is simply to ask people who live in a region whether they believe it to be mountainous.

The Himalayan Mountains of Nepal.

12

Across the world, in the shadow of the Himalayas, people have a very different view of what makes a mountain. An old story tells of a British climber who asked a local guide the names of several peaks more than 11,500 feet (3,505 m) high. The guide shrugged and told him that they were just foothills with no names. In this area, a mountain has to be pretty impressive just to be noticed.

Ama Dablam, a mountain in Nepal's Himalayas.

What powerful forces build mountains? Are mountains still forming today? To answer these questions, we have to start by looking at the largest solid parts of the earth, the continents and the ocean floors, which make up what we call the earth's *Crust*. The crust lies atop a thick fluid region called the earth's *Mantle*. Beneath the mantle lies the region called the *Core*, which extends all the way to the center of the earth.

The volcano Farallon de Pajaros
of the Mariana Islands, Micronesia.

According to the theory of *Plate Tectonics*, the surface of the earth is divided into large blocks known as plates. These plates may include both continental and oceanic crust and can be thousands of miles wide. Most scientists agree that there are seven major plates and about eighteen minor ones.

Driven by forces deep within the earth, the plates slowly move across the mantle at the rate of about 1 or 2 centimeters a year. This movement provides much of the energy needed for mountain building.

The San Andreas Fault in California.

There are three main types of mountains, classified by the way they form: folded mountains, fault-block mountains, and volcanoes. *Folded Mountains* form when crustal plates collide, subjecting large regions to immense pressure. Over thousands or even millions of years, this pressure can fold huge blocks of rock and sediment into spectacular mountain ranges. The rock layers can be bent into mild waves or violently deformed into accordionlike patterns, such as the sharp ridges of the North American Rocky Mountains.

Banff National Park, Alberta, Canada: The folded limestone layers of the Rocky Mountains.

Fault-Block Mountains form along faults, which are fractures in the earth's crust. Faults should not be confused with plate boundaries (although many faults do occur at plate boundaries). A single tectonic plate may contain thousands of faults. Within the plates, faults divide large blocks of crust. As stress builds up, these large blocks may move along the fault. The energy released by this movement is a major cause of earthquakes. The different blocks can move side to side, up and down, or they can even tilt and rotate. Fault-block mountains form when one block rises or falls (or both) in relation to its neighbor. The Sierra Nevada Range in the western United States is a classic example of fault-block mountains.

Sequoia National Park, California:
Mt. Whitney of the Sierra Nevada.

19

Volcanoes form when hot gases and molten rock, called *Magma,* erupt onto the earth's surface by way of a vent, or hole. After magma reaches the surface, it is called *Lava.* Lava may exit the vent in several different ways: it can flow out as a liquid; it can explode from the vent as solid particles; or it can be ejected from the vent as a combination of both solid particles and liquid. Cooling lava piles up around the vent, forming a volcanic mountain.

Unlike folded and fault-block mountains, which can take thousands or even millions of years to form, volcanoes can form very quickly. One day in 1943 a volcano named Parícutin emerged in the middle of a farmer's field in Mexico. Within one week it was 460 feet (140 m) high, and within a year it attained official mountain status by growing to a height of 1,065 feet (325 m).

The fiery eruption of a volcano in the Philippines.

Volcanoes also may lie dormant for centuries and suddenly explode one day with tremendous force. The 1980 eruption of Mount St. Helens in Washington blew away the entire side of the mountain, producing the largest landslide ever seen. While its eruption had been predicted, the sheer magnitude of the destruction took everyone by surprise. Sixty-one people were killed or reported missing. The blast leveled forests as far away as 17 miles (27 km). Hundreds of square miles were devastated. The explosion shot ash 12 miles (19 km) into the sky, where it spread and then fell over much of eastern Washington, northern Idaho, and western Montana.

The eruption of Mt. St. Helens.
Inset: The Toutle River channel winds through layers
of lightweight volcanic rock called pumice.

No matter how mountains are formed, their presence helps shape a region's climate. Air moving toward a mountain is deflected upward and rises. As air rises it cools, and any moisture it contains is likely to condense and fall as rain or snow. This is why the side of a mountain that faces the prevailing wind—the *Windward* side—often receives a great deal of rain or snow. The city of Cherrapunji, near the base of the Himalayas, receives one of the greatest annual rainfalls on earth—428 inches (1,087 cm)—on its windward side. It once received 41 inches (104 cm) of rain in a single day.

Chinook clouds of warm, moist air in the Canadian Rockies.

The side that faces away from the prevailing wind is called the *Leeward* side. Because the air has already dropped much of its moisture while rising up the windward side, the leeward side of a mountain usually receives much less rain or snow. This lack of moisture can extend across a wide area far beyond the mountain range; such a region is called a *Rain Shadow*. Many of the world's deserts lie in a rain shadow. The dryness of the Mojave Desert in the southwest United States is largely due to the Sierra Nevada Range directly to the west.

25

Mountain climates are notable for their tremendous diversity within a relatively small area. Increases in altitude result in a rapid drop in temperature. Air at higher altitudes is also less dense, allowing sunlight to pass through more easily than at lower elevations; thus, more heat energy hits the land surface. However, the thin mountain air cannot hold this heat energy, and the temperature drops rapidly in the absence of sunlight. This results in large temperature swings from day to night.

If the temperature is cold enough, mountain precipitation falls as snow. As the snow accumulates on the mountain, it can pile up to the point where it becomes unstable. This unstable snow can produce a devastating landslide called an *Avalanche*. The tons of ice and snow in an avalanche can destroy everything in its path. One avalanche that occurred during World War I in the Italian Alps killed more than 6,000 soldiers.

An avalanche scar in Rocky Mountain National Park, Colorado.
Inset: Sawtooth ridges in the mountains of Idaho.

If the temperature is cold throughout the year and the falling snow does not melt away during the warmer months, over time the snow can pile up and compress into massive blocks of ice called *Glaciers.* Many glaciers become large enough to flow under their own weight and slowly move downhill. Most glaciers move less than 3 feet (91 cm) per day. As they move, they shape and carve the land underneath, dramatically altering the mountain surface.

❧

Sometimes the glaciers form bowl-like depressions, called *Cirques,* on the sides of mountains. When several cirques connect, a sawtooth-shaped ridge forms. If the cirques carve their way inward around the sides of a mountain peak, the result can be a *Horn.* The famous Matterhorn in Switzerland was carved out of the mountain by cirques.

Bryn Mawr Glacier, Prince William Sound, Alaska.
Inset: The Matterhorn of the Swiss Alps.

Other forces, too, work steadily to wear down mountains. Flowing water forms tiny grooves that merge into small channels and finally into riverbeds and valleys. When water freezes in small fissures in mountain rock, it expands, cracking and weakening the rock. Wind causes erosion by scouring the rock surface with small grains of sand and dust. Roots of shrubs and trees gradually split apart mountain rock. Plantlike forms called lichens dissolve rock for nutrients and thus help create mountain soils.

Lichens on the rocks of Cadillac Mountain, Acadia National Park, Maine.

Because of the extreme weather conditions and the relatively young age of the mountain ecosystems, fewer species of plants and animals inhabit the higher elevations than exist in the plains and jungles below. Those that do use different strategies to survive. As trees approach the *Timberline* (the elevation above which trees cannot grow), they are stunted by the cold and wind and often resemble bushes more than trees. Plants that grow above the timberline tend to be small, with dark, fuzzy leaves, and grow close to the ground. These features help the plants hold in as much heat as possible.

Trees and bushes near the timberline are called krummholz, a German word for "crooked wood."

Insects and spiders, too, can tolerate the harsh mountain conditions. Some insect larvae can even survive being frozen and then thawed out. *Jumping Spiders* in the Himalayas live in the highest altitudes of any animals in the world. They have been seen living at 22,000 feet (6,706 m).

While an imposing mountain range may seem indestructible, the mountain environment is in reality extremely complex and easily disrupted—particularly when people become involved. Mountains are central to a myriad of human activities. Probably the least harmful of these is the well-managed grazing of domesticated animals such as sheep, goats, and cattle. In regions with harsh winters, this activity is seasonal. The animals graze the highlands in the summer and the lowlands in the winter. By moving the animals with the seasons, the herders give the environment time to recover.

Cows grazing in the alpine fields of Switzerland.

In contrast, growing crops in the mountains has a much greater impact on the environment. *Terracing* is a process used throughout the world to raise crops on steep slopes. By sculpting level rows on the mountainsides, farmers can plant and irrigate crops on otherwise unusable land. While terracing increases food production, it permanently changes the mountain landscape. Terraced farms are found mainly in the tropical mountains of the world, where the mild climate allows farming year-round.

Rice terraces in the Philippines.

38

Many other activities of modern civilization can harm the mountain ecosystems. Building dams for flood control or to produce electricity creates artificial lakes in what were previously valleys, permanently eliminating the plants and animals that lived there. Industries such as mining and forestry can scar the landscape, often damaging it beyond recovery. Pollution originating in the lowlands can be carried on the wind into the mountains, where it can harm the forests.

39

In addition to the effects of agriculture and industry, the fragile mountain environment can be overburdened by recreational visitors. Backpacking and camping, the construction of permanent tourist facilities, and pollution from automobiles all put stress on the delicate balance of life in the mountains. Ironically, the people who love mountains the most are sometimes contributing to their demise just by visiting.

Logging damage in Oregon.

To preserve *Mountains* for the generations to come, we must regulate our impact on them. We must continue to set aside mountain wilderness areas, and when we make use of mountains, we must practice thoughtful planning and management. While in the past these immense land masses have helped to control our destiny, we now are responsible for theirs.

The Adirondack Mountains, New York.

J